Jacob of Serugh, the Man Behind the Mimre

Analecta Gorgiana

1044

Series Editor

George Anton Kiraz

Jacob of Serugh, the Man Behind the Mimre

Khalid Dinno

gorgias press

2011

Gorgias Press LLC, 954 River Road, Piscataway, NJ, 08854, USA

www.gorgiaspress.com

Copyright © 2011 by Gorgias Press LLC

Originally published in 2010

2011 ܐܒ

ﮒ

ISBN 978-1-4632-0092-3   ISSN 1935-6854

Reprinted from the 2010 Piscataway edition.

Printed in the United States of America

JACOB OF SERUGH,
THE MAN BEHIND THE MIMRE

KHALID DINNO

As we convene in this symposium to celebrate the heritage of this great church father, I have selected to speak of the man behind this immense heritage, a man whose learning and piety earned him esteem as the flute of the Holy Spirit and as harp of the Orthodox Church.

In his flag publication in Arabic, the book entitled *"Al Lulu al-Manthour" (The Scattered Pearls)*, Aphram Barsoum, himself a man of renowned eloquence, described Mor Jacob of Serugh in a manner that reflected deep admiration. In quoting from Barsoum some of Barsoum's eloquence of expression will be lost in the translation from Arabic, even when the translation is made by an experienced and eloquent scholar such as Matti Moosa. All the same, it is worthwhile to quote briefly from Moosa's translation:[1]

> ......Jacob's poetry contains masterpieces and beauties which astound the mind and arrest the heart. It is also characterized by immaculate style and perspicuity, exquisite themes, masterful expression and firm and clear form.
>
> ......The more he penetrated his poetical theme the more he enriches it with eloquence and beauty, and the more he creates new forms, delicate expressions and brilliant techniques, which drive away boredom and alert the reader that he is opposite a mighty ocean full of literary pearls and

---

[1] Barsoum, Ignatius Aphram I. *The Scattered Pearls, A History of Syriac Literature and Sciences*, transl. by Matti Moosa, 255, Gorgias Press, 2003.

uncommon objects… Thus his tongue was a spring of wisdom and he himself was one of the chosen of God and the most famous of the Saints of his time, the age of faith, heroism, and orthodox religious principles.

Mor Jacob epitomizes what we understand Syriac spirituality to characterize, namely the way of seeing and meditating upon God in a symbolic manner. This entails a kind of dual vision that sees simultaneously the visible physical world and the hidden realities of God concealed within it, which are conveyed through the Scriptures, Christ, the Church, the sacrament, by means of faith and the Holy Spirit. This way of seeing the Christian realities expressed itself best and most characteristically within the Syriac tradition of poetry. Mor Jacob's mimre, therefore, earned him fame and continue to assist those who seek to find the classical Syriac mode of understanding the Bible. The testimonies of Barhebraes and Jacob of Edessa together speak of 763 such homilies. Although Mor Jacob's greatest literary output was in the form of mimre, he also composed madrase, sogyatha and other genre of various compositions.

By means of the mimro genre, Mor Jacob weaves exegetical comment, imaginative and dramatic dialogue in order to unfold an event. We must be mindful of the difference between the literary genre as utilized by Jacob of Serugh and other Syriac authors and between the styles of expression of Greek and Latin writers. In this respect I can do no better than quote Sebastian Brock, where in *Baptismal Themes* he says:[2]

> I should stress at the outset that it is essential to read Jacob on his own terms, and not approach him with our own Western European presuppositions, if we are to appreciate his true originality and profoundity. In other words we must make an effort of the imagination in order to recapture this supra-historical way of thinking.

---

[2] Brock, S.P. *Baptismal Themes in the Writings of Jacob of Serugh*, 325–6, OCA, 205, 1978.

Hence the culture and taste for whom Mor Jacob wrote are important and must be given due consideration.

One of the most significant themes that come through again and again in his mimre is the economy of salvation. This theme is centered on the mystery of the Son of God who became tangibly revealed in his Incarnation. Hence, the words and deeds of the incarnate Son of God are replete with hidden realities and powers. By a holistic vision of the entire Biblical history, Mor Jacob views the path of divine economy for the redemption of humanity. His mimre reflect a profound conviction on the central position of Christ through the Bible, often displayed through images and types. It is Christ who inspires and leads the prophets; all the prophecies are like lamps that illuminate the earth through the coming of Christ, the Sun. All the prophets and prophecies are like rivers flowing to the same ocean with their own parts of inspiration.

As poet and pastor, Mor Jacob propounds the mystery of Christ through his symbolic-typological vision; one that steers him away from disputes and investigations, proclaiming that the Holy Spirit inspires the faithful with the knowledge of the Truth.

Mor Jacob calls himself a "harp" on which the fingers of the Holy Spirit play on. His mimre reveal a man who felt he was duty bound to devote his entire creative energy to express and proclaim the majesty of God, the Omnipotent and Creator. There is an abundance of examples showing his genuine and frank nature, his spontaneity, honesty and readiness to admit failure. His mimre reflect various moods and emotions, often with more than one mood appearing in one mimro; feeling of inadequacy, self approach, self pity, and humility on the one hand, and self confidence, pride and assertiveness, on the other. In the one mimro you may see him show humility and compassion, but also readiness to admonish those who are not attentive to hear what he has to say. He opens up his heart to his listeners and readers, and is always ready to express his inner feelings without pretence or camouflage. His treatment of difficult subjects at times shows duality of thought even a touch of enigma. He often complains of inadequacy and frustration at not being able to find the right word or expression, beseeching the Lord for forgiveness and inspiration so that he may shed away laziness and march on towards the task to which he considered himself destined and ordained; the task of revealing and glorifying the Creator and Savior.

SELECTED SAMPLES FROM JACOB'S MIMRE:[3]

The following are selected samples from a number of mimre which show the the various facets that make up Mor Jacob's creative personality.

On His Feeling of Inadequacy

This is a feeling Mor Jacob often expresses in his mimre. In it he shares with his audience the challenge, even the agony of finding the words that would befit the subject he is addressing. Examples: [4]

V1, p36, L4+5

ܫܪܒܐ ܥܫܝܢ ܘܡܚܝܠ ܗܘܢܐ ܘܡܢ ܐܗܘܐ:
ܢܫܩܠܐ ܟܒܪ ܕܝܠܝ ܫܘܪܝܐ ܐܝܬܝܐ ܬܫܥܝܬܝ܀

M 2:337 — The story is difficult and the mind weak, what is to be done? For if it wasn't for the weakness of my mind, I would have, in fact, started to speak.

V2, p861, L5+6

ܡܢ ܕܝܢ ܢܬܠ ܠܝ ܨܒܥܐ ܡܗܝܪܬܐ ܕܫܠܝܚܘܬܐ:
ܕܒܟܢܪܐ ܕܬܠܡܝܕܘܬܐ ܠܚܪܬܐ ܐܙܡܪ܀

M 68:30 — Would I have the Apostle's skilful fingers to sing with the Disciplehood's harp, about the end!

V2, p861, L7+8

ܡܚܝܠܐ ܐܢܐ ܕܐܡܪ ܥܠ ܗܘ ܕܝܢܐ ܪܒܐ ܕܥܬܝܕ:
ܦܘܠܘܣ ܢܐܬܐ ܘܗܘ ܢܠܦ ܠܢ ܫܪܝܪܬܐ܀

M 68:31 — I am too weak to speak about the coming great Judgment: let Paul teach us the truthful facts.

V3, p631, L4+5

ܐܢܐ ܒܪܢܫܐ ܠܐ ܡܫܟܚܐ ܘܠܐ ܙܕܩܐ:
ܘܠܐ ܡܛܝ ܐܢܐ ܠܡܬܢܝܘ ܠܒܪ ܐܠܗܐ܀

---

[3] Bedjan, P., ed. *Homiliae Selectae Mar Jacobi Serughensis*, Vols. I–V, Paris/Leipzig, 1905–10. Republished with additional material by Sebastian P. Brock by Gorgias Press, 2006.

[4] The mimre are referenced here by mimro number and line.

M 94:515 — I, the inadequate one, am neither wise nor learned and do not know how to investigate on the Son of God.

V1, p48, L8+9
ܘܒܚܣܝܪܘܬܐ ܐܬܡܠܠ ܠܝ ܫܪܒܗ ܕܡܘܫܐ:
ܠܐ ܡܪܝ ܬܛܥܐ ܠܥܡܠܗ ܕܚܘܪܐ ܕܡܚܝܠܐ܀

M 3:106 — As the story of Moses has been told only incompletely by me, Lord, don't forget this idler's menial effort.

V1, p48, L10+11
ܠܒܨܝܪܘܬܗ ܕܡܐܡܪܐ ܩܒܠ ܡܪܚܡܢܐܝܬ:
ܘܢܦܠ ܡܥܘܢ ܥܠ ܦܬܘܪܟ ܦܝܣܐܝܬ܀

M 3:107 — Accept with compassion the inadequacy of my mimro, and let my coin fall on your table with favor.

V1, p48, L12+13
ܕܠܐ ܡܬܚܝܒܢܐ ܠܐ ܕܬܚܡܬܟ ܡܪܝ ܡܢ ܟܐܢܘܬܐ:
ܡܢ ܓܝܪ ܡܨܐ ܕܢܣܬܟܠܟ ܢܐܡܪ ܫܪܒܟ܀

M 3:108 — My Lord, I should not be blamed by the Justice for I never defined you, for who can speak of you sufficiently and limit you?

V1, p48, L14+15
ܩܒܠ ܕܫܝܐ ܕܩܠܐ ܙܥܘܪܐ ܕܫܕܪ ܠܫܢܝ:
ܘܛܪ ܠܝ ܠܟܘܢ ܣܝܡܬܐ ܕܪܚܡܐ ܥܕ ܐܬܐ ܐܢܐ܀

M 3:109 — Accept as gift the few tunes that my tongue has sent forth and preserve for me the treasure of mercies until I come to you.

V1, p48, L16+17
ܚܠܦ ܟܪܝܘܬܐ ܕܙܡܪܬ ܗܪܟܐ ܒܡܚܝܠܘܬܐ:
ܢܩܘܡܘܢ ܪܚܡܝܟ ܘܒܗܘܢ ܐܚܐ ܢܨܚܢܐܝܬ܀

M 3:110 — In exchange for what I have sung briefly and feebly here, may your mercies endure so that I may live through them to eternity.

V2, p77, L1+2

ܐܬܬܥܝܪ ܟܢܪܝ ܘܙܡܪ ܫܘܒܚܐ ܦܪܘܫܐܝܬ:

ܠܒܪܐ ܒܩ̈ܠܐ ܣܓܝ̈ܐܐ ܫܘܒܚܐ ܡܠܝܐܝܬ܀

M 65:1 — Wake up my harp and recite outstanding praise for the Son with many tunes, full of glory.

The feeling of inadequacy is at times mixed with a feeling of self admonition, even reprimand:

V2, p77, L17+ V2,p78,L1

ܥܕ ܩܝܡ ܐܝܬܝܟ ܐܬܬܥܝܪ ܫܒܚ ܐܘ ܥܛܠܐ:

ܒܟܠ ܡܕܡ ܓܝܪ ܙܒܢܐ ܐܝܬ ܠܗ ܘܗܫܐ ܐܘܕܐ܀

M 35:9 — O, you idle one, while still alive, wake up and praise, for there is time for every thing and so profess (God) now.

V2, p78, L2+3

ܥܕܠܐ ܢܐܬܐ ܡܘܬܐ ܘܢܫܪܐ ܡܢ ܒܢܝܢܟ:

ܘܢܦܣܘܩ ܡ̈ܢܬܐ ܡܡܠܠܢ̈ܝܬܐ ܡܢ ܬܫܒܘܚܬܐ܀

M 35:10 — Before death arrives to undo your body structure, breaking the strings that utter praise.

V2, p78, L4+5

ܥܕܠܐ ܢܕܪܘܟ ܫܬܩܗ ܕܡܘܬܐ ܠܦܘܡܐ ܒܫܝܘܠ:

ܘܢܫܬܩܝܘܗܝ ܩ̈ܠܐ ܡܢ ܠܡܫܪܐ ܕܡܫܒܚܢ ܗܘܘ܀

M 35:11 — Before the silence of death reaches the mouth in Sheol to silence the mouth that utters praising hymns.

Elsewhere reverting to self pity and the feeling of inadequacy, seeking refuge in God's mercy:

V3, p826, L7+8

ܙܥܘܪܐ ܕܐܣܘܬܝ ܡܠܬܝ ܫܝܛܐ ܘܐܢܐ ܡܚܝܠ:

ܘܠܐܝܢܐ ܫܘܚܢܐ ܐܙܠ ܗܫܐ ܠܡܣܒܪܘ܀

M 102:22 — The dressings are few, my word is despised and I am feeble, so now to which of my wounds do I tend?

V3, p844, L19+20

M 103:27 — Silence, o wretched one, for your word is despised,
you are feeble, the wound is incurable and the pain
is a challenge to the healer.

V5, p855, L11+12

M 192:202 — May your compassion be the defender of my
weakness when you rise (for Judgment) and may it
approach you on my behalf.

V5, p855, L13+14

M 192:203 — Let it speak to you loudly about my misery so that
with your Grace you may bring life to this
undeserving weakling.

V5, p855, L15+16

M192:204 — Who is this inadequate one? And what are his
defects? Do not descend toward this weakling to
judge him.

V5, p855, L17+18

M192:205 — Do not waste your great Judgment on this
insignificant one, cast your vengeance upon the
infidels who did not believe in you.

V5, p855, L19+20

M 192:206 — It is an insult to you if you were to enter into
judgment with this who is worthless and whose
sins are trivial.

V5, p856, L1+2

M 192:207 — Let us assume that he is all sins, who is he and
what can be his sins to merit your revenge?

V5, p856, L3+4

M 192:208 — Let your mercy utter these words to you on my
behalf so that I may live in grace, and your mercy
will shine in me.

On Assertiveness and Confidence

V1, p270, L11+12

M 12:28 — For me, who is free, the praise is beautiful, if I
distinctly understand that my will is directed to
cease or else live for praise.

V1, p270, L13+14

M 12:29 — If I stopped, I would be punished by the Justice,
for it requires the free men to praise with
distinction.

*Yet he goes on in the next stanza to express profound reverence towards the
Creator saying:*

V1, p270, L15+16

M 12:30 — Therefore, O Lord, I praise you with fear, for, although I am undeserving, I still dare and am incapable.

V4, p87, L12+13

ܒܟܠ ܛܠܠܐ ܘܨܘܪܐ ܓܘܫܡܐ ܕܟܠܗ ܩܢܘܡܐ:

ܘܠܡܣܬܟܠ ܓܠܝܢ ܐܢܝܢ ܟܠ ܕܐܡܪ ܐ̱ܢܐ܀

M 109:273 — There is the shadow and there is the tangible (aspect) of every reality, and all that of which I say is clear for those who understand.

V4, p87, L14+15

ܒ̈ܢܝ ܐ̱ܪ̈ܙܐ ܕܐܦ ܒܓܠܝܐ ܡܠܬܝ ܒܥܐ ܠܡܩܒܠܘܬܗ:

ܬܪ̈ܥܝܬܐ ܕܡܣܬܟܠܝܢ ܠܗ ܢܩܒܠܘܢܗ܀

M 109:274 — My word, despite its clarity, requires the sons of sacrament and scholars to accept it clearly.

V4, p135, L22 (bottom line)+p136, L1

ܠܐܝܢܐ ܕܨܒܐ ܐܘܕܗ ܒܚܘܒܐ ܠܗ ܐܡܪ ܐ̱ܢܐ:

ܠܐ̱ܚܪ̈ܢܐ ܕܝܢ ܫܬܩܐ ܚܠܐ ܐ̱ܢܐ ܡܛܠ ܦܘܪܫܐ܀

M 112:31 — I talk with love to whoever listens; and with others I adhere to silence for a purpose.

V4, p136, L2+3

ܫܬܩܐ ܪܒܐ ܚܫܘܒ ܠܡܠܬܝ. ܐܘ ܕܠܐ ܚܘܒ:

ܟܠܚܕ ܡܬܘܡ ܠܐ ܬܛܥܢ ܠܟ ܡܕܡ ܕܡܬܐܡܪ܀

M 112:32 — You who do not have love, count my word as great silence and do not ever carry burden of what is told to you.

V4, p136, L4+5

ܐܝܬ ܗ̱ܘ ܐ̱ܢܫܐ ܕܚܦܝܛ ܢܡܠܠ ܡܚܒܒܐܝܬ:

ܘܠܗ ܐܡܪ ܐ̱ܢܐ ܘܫܬܩ ܐ̱ܢܐ ܠܟ ܟܕ ܡܚܒ ܐ̱ܢܐ܀

M 112:33 — The one who is anxious to speak with love, to him I speak; but for you I will keep quiet, whilst still loving (you).

V4, p136, L10+11

ܢܘܟܪܝܐ ܓܝܪ ܡܡܠܠܘܬܐ ܗܕܐ ܒܐܘܪܚܗ:

ܘܐܠܐ ܐܚܕܗ ܐ̱ܝܟ ܒܥܝܬܐ ܠܐ ܗܘܐ ܙܪܘܩܗ܀

M 112:36 — Teaching goes on along its way with humility, and
it would not reside with him, he who does not
aspire to grasp it.

On Supplication

Almost invariably the opening lines of his mimre are
supplications for illumination, to help him find the path to the
truth he wants to express to his audience:

V1, p49, L1+2

M 4:1 — O, Son of God, your mimre took me down to the
deep seas of your mysteries, but with you I was
rescued from the waves that surround me.

V1, p49, L3+4

M 4:2 — The waves of your discourses beleaguered me
greatly; you are the sailor, take me to the port of
truth.

V2, p77, L1+2

M 35:1 — Wake up, my harp, and praise the Son with
distinction, with many tunes full of love.

V2, p77, L9+10

M 35:5 — Praise externally with the five senses of the body,
and praise in secret with the five senses of the
spirit.

V2, p77, L11+12

M 35:6 — With smell, touch, taste, hearing and sight-with these five sense, praise with your body.

V2, p77, L13+14

ܘܐܦ ܒܡܕܥܐ ܘܒܡܣܘܟܠܐ ܘܒܡܣܘܪܥܢܐ:

ܘܗܘܢܐ ܘܡܚܫܒܬܐ ܒܪ̈ܓܫܘܗ̇ ܟܣ̈ܝܐ ܕܢܦܫܐ ܐܘܕܐ܀

M 35:7 — And then praise with the hidden senses of the soul: knowledge, understanding, awareness, mind and thought.

V4, p61, L6+5 from the bottom

ܗܢܐ ܠܫܢܝ ܗܘ ܡܣܟܢܬܐ ܢܠܐܐ ܫܪܒܟ:

ܐܝܟ ܐܒܪܗܡ ܕܡܣܟܐ ܗܘܐ ܕܢܚܙܐ ܝܘܡܟ܀

M 109:3 — Here is my miserable tongue longing to tell your story, as Abraham longed to see your day.

V4, p61, L4+3 from the bottom

ܘܐܢ ܙܕܝܩܐ ܚܙܟ ܗܘܐ ܒܐܡܪܐ ܘܚܕܝ ܗܘ ܒܟ:

ܐܢܐ ܒܨܝܪܐ ܒܡܐܡܪܐ ܐܚܙܝܟ ܘܐܬܒܣܡ ܒܟ܀

M 109:4 — And if the Virtuous One had seen you in the lamb and rejoiced in you, I the inadequate one, see you in the mimro and rejoice in you.

V4, p61, bottom two lines

ܚܕܝ ܐܒܪܗܡ ܒܐܡܪܐ ܕܐܪ̈ܙܝܟ ܕܪܫܝܡ ܗܘܐ ܒܗ:

ܚܕܝ ܐܦ ܠܝ ܒܡܐܡܪܐ ܕܫܘܦܪܟ ܡܡܠܠ ܒܗ܀

M 109:5 — Abraham was glad with the lamb that signified your mysteries, bring me joy, with a mimro that shows your beauty.

V5, p117, L1+2

ܦܬܚ ܡܪܝ ܣܦܘ̈ܬܝ ܕܐܟܪܙ ܣܘܓܐܐ ܕܒܣܝܡܘܬܟ:

ܘܐܥܒܪ ܒܠܫܢܝ ܡܐܡܪ ܫܘܒܚܐ ܕܐܠܗܘܬܟ܀

M 154:1 — O Lord, open my lips to herald your abundant sweetness, and pass through my tongue the mimro of your glorious divinity.

V5, p117, L3+4

ܗܒ ܠܝ ܕܐܗܘܐ ܩܠܐ ܠܡܡܠܠܘ ܩܕܝܫܘܬܟ:

ܘܒܗ ܐܫܡܥ ܙܘܗܐ ܕܚܝ̈ܝ ܩܕܝܫܘܬܟ܀

M 154:2 — Help me to be the diligent agent of your word so that through it I may end with virtue the journey of my life.

V5, p117, L11+12

ܗܐ ܡܘܗܒ ܠܟ ܦܘܡܝ ܢܗܘܐ ܠܟܢܪܐ ܩܢܝ ܩܠܐ:
ܘܢܥܘܠ ܡܠܬܟ ܢܡܠܠ ܒܗ ܟܕ ܠܐ ܫܘܐ܀

M 154:6 — My mouth is given to you, let it be the harp for the tunes of your tidings, so let your word enter to speak through it, even though it does not deserve.

V5, p117, L13+14

ܒܡܘܢ ܫܘܐ ܦܘܡܐ ܕܛܢܦܐ ܠܡܛܐ ܠܟ:
ܐܠܐ ܒܪ̈ܚܡܝܟ ܕܐܦ ܥܠ ܒܝ̈ܫܐ ܡܪܣܣܝܢ ܐܢܘܢ܀

M 154:7 — How does a soiled mouth deserve to reach out to you, if not through your mercies that are endowed even upon the wicked?

On faith and salvation

This is the core theme in many of Mor Jacob's Mimre. Like St. Ephrem before him, Mor Jacob abhorred the notion of analyzing the Father and the Son and derided those who were engaged in it. He found refuge in faith, away from the pitfalls of philosophical discourses:

V3, p587, L7+8

ܗܒ ܠܝ ܡܪܢ ܐܬܪܗܒ ܒܟ ܟܕ ܣܓܕ ܐ̱ܢܐ:
ܘܠܐ ܐܒܩܐ ܡܘܠܕܟ ܟܕ ܗܓܐ ܐ̱ܢܐ܀

M 94:57 — Our lord, grant me that I may express awe and kneel before you and not investigate your birth, when I meditate it.

V3, p587, L9+10

ܦܫܛܬ ܒܨܝܬܟ ܘܒܚܘ̈ܡܐ ܠܐ ܐܫܟܚܬܟ:
ܘܐܣܝܬ ܠܚܘܣܢܐ ܕܗܝܡܢܘܬܐ ܘܐܫܟܚܬܟ ܠܟ܀

M 94:58 — I wandered, scrutinizing you, and could not find you among the limiting definitions, so I took refuge in faith and I found you.

V3, p587, L11+12

ܢܦܩܬ ܐܒܥܝܟ ܥܡ ܚܟܝܡܐ ܘܐܬܬܩܠܬ ܒܟ:

ܘܦܢܝܬ ܗܠܟܬ ܥܡ ܗܕܝܘܛܐ ܘܠܐ ܐܬܬܩܠܬ܀

M 94:59 — I set out to search for you amongst the wise and I stumbled, then I walked with the simple, without stumbling.

V3, p587, L13+14

ܡܢ ܨܝܕܝ ܕܢܘܢܐ ܝܠܦܬ ܗܝܡܢܘܬܐ:

ܘܚܟܡܬ ܥܠܡܐ ܠܗܝܡܢܘܬܐ ܠܐ ܡܬܒܥܝܐ܀

M 94:60 — I learned faith from the fishermen; the wisdom of the world is not needed for faith.

V3, p587, L15+16

ܡܢܗ̇ ܕܗܘܐ ܚܟܡܬ ܥܠܡܐ ܢܦܠܘ ܣܓܝܐܐ:

ܘܟܕ ܒܨܝܢ ܠܗ ܠܒܪ ܐܠܗܐ ܢܦܠܘ ܡܢ ܪܘܡܗ܀

M 94:61 — Through the wisdom of the world many fell, and whilst scrutinizing about the Son of God they fell before his majesty.

V3, p630, L20+p631, L1

ܐܢܐ ܡܡܬܘܡ ܟܠ ܕܐܠܗܐ ܗܘ ܝܕܥ ܐܢܐ ܠܗ:

ܘܠܐ ܒܥܬܐ ܕܒܪ ܐܠܗܐ ܗܘ ܡܗܝܡܢ ܐܢܐ ܠܗ܀

M 94:513 — I know he is ever God, and I believe without a search that he is the Son of God.

V3, p631, L2+3

ܐܝܬ ܗܘ ܡܠܦܢܐ ܘܐܝܬ ܚܟܝܡܐ ܘܕܪܘܫܐ:

ܘܐܝܬ ܝܘܢܝܐ ܘܐܝܬ ܕܣܡܝܟܝܢ ܥܠ ܝܕܥܬܐ܀

M 94:514 — There are the teachers, there are the wise, and the inquisitors and the Greeks, and there are those who rely on scholarship.

V3, p631, L4+5

ܐܢܐ ܒܨܝܪܐ ܠܐ ܚܟܝܡܐ ܘܠܐ ܕܪܘܫܐ:

ܘܠܐ ܝܕܥ ܐܢܐ ܠܡܒܨܝܘܬܗ ܒܒܪ ܐܠܗܐ܀

M 94:515 — I, the inadequate one, am neither a wise man nor a learned one, and I do not know how to scrutinize about the Son of God.

V3, p631, L6+7

ܠܝ ܐܠܗܐ ܗܘ ܕܝܠܝܕ ܒܒܣܪ: ܡܢ ܒܝܬ ܕܘܝܕ:

ܐܦ ܟܕ ܩܐܡ ܒܚܫܗ ܚܫܐ ܕܙܩܝܦܘܬܐ܀

M 94:516 — For me, He is God, born in the flesh, from the house of David, even as He suffered on the Cross.

V3, p631, L8+9

ܘܡܐ ܕܚܟܝܡܐ ܡܬܚܫܒܝܢ ܥܠ ܫܪܒܗ ܠܐ ܩܪܒ ܐܢܐ:

ܠܝ ܓܝܪ ܡܐ ܠܝ ܕܗܕܝܘܛܐ ܐܢܐ ܥܡ ܚܟܝܡܐ܀

M 94:517 — When the wise discuss his news I do not go near to them, for what is it to me, the ignorant one, to be with the wise?

V3, p631, L10+11

ܘܡܐ ܕܡܬܚܫܒܝܢ ܣܦܪܐ ܫܪܒܗ ܝܕܥ ܐܢܐ ܐܫܬܩ:

ܕܡܢܟܪ ܐܢܐ ܗܘ ܡܢ ܣܦܪܘܬܐ ܘܚܟܡܬܐ܀

M 94:518 — When the learned discuss his news, I know how to remain quiet, for I am a stranger to scholarship and wisdom.

V3, p631, L12+13

ܘܡܐ ܕܕܪܫܝܢ ܒܗ ܝܕܘܥܬܐ ܠܐ ܫܡܥ ܐܢܐ:

ܠܐ ܣܡܝܟ ܐܢܐ ܓܝܪ ܥܠ ܝܕܥܬܐ ܕܒܨܝܐ ܠܒܪܐ܀

M 94:519 — When the scholars argue about him, I do not listen, for I do not rely on the scholarship that examines the Son.

V3, p631, L14+15

ܘܐܡܬܝ ܕܒܥܝܢ ܕܢܦܠܓܘܢܝܗܝ ܠܝܚܝܕܝܐ:

ܣܟܠܐ ܗܘ ܣܓܝ ܘܡܢܐ ܡܡܠܠܝܢ ܠܐ ܝܕܥ ܐܢܐ܀

M 94:520 — And whenever they want to dissect the Only begotten One, I become very stupid and fail to understand what they say.

V3, p631, L16+17

ܘܐܡܬܝ ܕܠܒܥܝܢ ܦܠܘܓܘܬܗ ܗܘܝܬ ܠܝ ܕܘܚܠܐ:

ܠܐ ܓܝܪ ܐܝܟ ܠܝ ܐܘܪܚܐ ܕܡܥܠܐ ܦܘܫܩܗܘܢ܀

M 94:521 — And whenever they deny His Incarnation I become deaf and will have no ears to hear their explanations.

V3, p631, L18+19
ܒܗܘ ܕܝܢ ܕܐܡܪ ܕܠܗ ܠܐܠܗܐ ܐܠܐ ܕܪܡܫܐ:
ܠܗ ܠܫܢܐ ܕܝܠܗ ܝܠܦܬ ܐܡܠܠ ܠܗܘ܀

M 94:522 — I never learnt to speak the language of those who say, God was not on the Cross.

V3, p631, L20+21
ܘܐܝܢܐ ܕܣܒܪ ܕܡܫܡܠܝܐܝܬ ܝܕܥܗ ܠܒܪܐ:
ܠܝ ܢܘܟܪܝܐ ܗܘ ܡܛܠ ܕܐܢܐ ܠܐ ܝܕܥ ܐܢܐ܀

M 94:523 — And whoever thinks he has known the Son precisely he is a stranger to me, for I know not.

V3, p632, L1+2
ܒܗܘ ܠܫܢܐ ܕܝܠܦ ܟܠܢܫ ܒܗ ܗܘ ܡܡܠܠ:
ܕܝܠܗ ܒܠܫܢܗ ܗܐ ܟܡ ܒܒܠ ܕܦܘܠܓܐ܀

M 94:524 — He speaks in the language that each one learnt in his own dialect, as in the time of Babylon.

V3, p632, L3+4
ܒܒܪ ܐܠܗܐ ܒܗܘ ܠܫܢܐ ܕܗܝܡܢܘܬܐ:
ܡܡܠܠ ܐܢܐ ܠܗ ܘܠܐ ܝܕܥ ܐܢܐ ܐܚܪܢܐ ܡܕܡ܀

M 94:525 — I speak about the Son of God with the language of faith and I know nothing else.

V3, p632, L5+6
ܘܡܠܦܢܐ ܕܐܝܬ ܗܘ ܒܥܠܡܐ ܚܟܝܡܐ ܐܘ ܡܦܫܩܢܐ:
ܘܡܦܩܩܢܐ ܡܡܠܠ ܟܠܢܫ ܐܝܟ ܝܕܥܬܗ܀

M 94:526 — There are no teachers, wise men or interpreters; everyone speaks according to his knowledge.

V3, p632, L7+8
ܝܕܥܬܐ ܕܡܛܝ ܥܕܡܐ ܠܗܢܐ ܕܢܕܥ ܫܠܡܬ:
ܕܐܘܕܥ ܐܢܐ ܕܠܐ ܡܬܡܠܠ ܒܪ ܐܠܗܐ܀

M 94:527 — My knowledge advanced to this extent: it is to know that the Son of God cannot be described.

V3, p632, L9+10

ܕܪܓܐ ܐܚܪܢܐ ܠܐ ܒܥܐ ܐܢܐ ܒܦܣܘܥܬܗ:

ܝܕܥܬ ܠܝ ܓܝܪ ܕܐܦ ܒܥܐ ܐܢܐ ܠܐ ܡܫܟܚ ܐܢܐ܀

M 94:528 — I do not want to rise another step for I have known that even if I wanted to, I could not.

V3, p632, L11+12

ܠܐ ܪܗܛ ܐܢܐ ܐܚܘܕ ܪܘܚܐ ܒܦܣܘܥܬܐ:

ܡܛܠ ܕܝܕܥܬ ܕܐܦ ܪܗܛ ܐܢܐ ܠܐ ܡܕܪܟ ܐܢܐ܀

M 94:529 — I do not run to catch the wind in steps, for I have come to know that even if I did I could not.

V3, p632, L13+14

ܠܐ ܡܡܪܚ ܐܢܐ ܐܥܘܠ ܝܡܐ ܘܐܡܢܐ ܚܠܗ:

ܝܕܥ ܐܢܐ ܓܝܪ ܒܟܘܠܬܗ ܕܡܢܘ ܡܟܝܠ ܡܟܝܠܐ܀

M 94:530 — I dare not fathom the sea and count its sand, for I know by whose hand it was measured.

V3, p632, L15+16

ܠܐ ܪܓܝܓ ܐܢܐ ܕܢܘܪܐ ܠܡܓܫ ܠܫܠܗܒܝܬܐ ܠܡܩܪܒ:

ܘܠܐ ܦܓܪܐ ܠܝ ܕܡܣܬܪܕ ܐܢܐ ܗܘ ܠܢܘܪܐ ܛܒ܀

M 94:531 — I do not aspire to touch the fire and the flame, for I have a body that greatly fears the fire.

V3, p633, L4+5

ܡܪܝ ܡܘܗܒܬܐ ܕܡܠܝܐ ܢܘܗܪܐ ܗܒ ܠܝ ܡܪܝ:

ܕܐܕܥ ܐܢܐ ܕܠܐ ܝܕܥ ܐܢܐ ܒܒܘܚܢܗ ܕܒܪܐ܀

M 94:536 — O Lord gave me a gift full of light, to know that I do not know how to test the Son.

V3, p633, L6+7

ܐܒܘܗܝ ܝܕܥ ܠܗ ܐܝܟ ܕܐܦ ܗܘ ܠܐܒܐ ܝܕܥ:

ܫܘܒܚܐ ܠܐܒܐ ܕܝܕܥ ܠܒܪܐ ܕܠܐ ܡܬܒܨܐ܀

M 94:537 — His father knows him just as He knows his Father, glory be to the Father who knows the Son, who is beyond examination.

On the Virtues of Silence

V2, p155, L17+18

ܒܕܘܟܬܐ ܕܐܠܨܐ ܠܡܡܠܠܘ ܦܘܡܗ ܐܛܡ:

ܐܝܢܐ ܕܫܪܪܐ ܒܕܝܠܗ ܗܘ ܡܣܠܝ ܡܢ ܟܐܢܘܬܐ܀

M 37:187 — Whoever refrains from speaking the truth in the right place is despised and rejected by the Justice.

V2, p155, L19+20

ܘܒܕܘܟܬܐ ܕܒܥܝܐ ܕܢܫܬܩ ܒܗ ܐܢ ܗܘ ܕܡܡܠܠ:

ܦܘܡܗ ܠܚܘܣܪܢܐ ܡܥܠܐ ܠܗ ܐܠܐ ܟܠܗ܀

M 37:188 — If he spoke where he must be silent, he will bring losses to himself.

On being Open and Transparent with his Audience

V5, p749, L1+2

ܪ̈ܢܝܢ ܚܫܝܠܐ ܡܥܝܪܢܝ ܠܟ ܡܪܝ ܕܐܡܠܠ ܓܝܘܪܓܝܣ:

ܬܘܩܦܐ ܐܒܥܐ ܡܢ ܐܠܗܘܬܟ ܕܐܫܬܥܐ ܬܫܥܝܬܗ܀

M 181:14 — My feeble mind urges me to write a mimro on St. George; in you I seek strength to narrate the story.

V5, p749, L3+4

ܗܐ ܡܥܝܪܝܢ ܠܝ ܬܪܝܢ ܚܘܫܒܝܢ ܠܡܟܬܒܘܬܗܘܢ:

ܘܚܕ ܚܕ ܡܢܗܘܢ ܠܘܬܗ ܢܓܕ ܘܡܩܛܪ ܠܝ܀

M 181:15 — Here are two ideas that urge me to write; each attracts me to it, forcibly.

V5, p749, L5+6

ܚܕ ܡܕܚܠ ܠܝ ܕܡܢ ܪܒܘܬܗ ܕܡܐܡܪܐ ܐܥܪܘܩ:

ܘܚܕ ܪܡܙ ܠܝ ܕܬܢܝ ܫܪܒܗ ܘܠܐ ܬܕܚܠ܀

M 181:16 — One frightens me, and on account of the magnitude of the mimro I run away, and the other signaled to me: tell His story and do not be afraid!

V5, p749, L7+8

ܠܚܫܒܐ ܕܗܢܐ ܚܕ ܚܘܫܒܐ ܗܘ ܕܐܪܗܒܢܝ:

ܘܒܨܬ ܕܡܠܟܗ ܡܠܠ ܚܣܝܪܬܐ ܘܠܐ ܝܘܬܪܢܐ܀

M 181:17 — I questioned the idea that frightened me, and found its advice defective and of no benefits.

V5, p749, L9+10

M 181:18 — I followed the one that encouraged me to
approach the amazing mimro, and found the
counsel that it gave me not without merit.

When he Likens himself to a Child

In several mimre Mor Jacob likens himself to a child muttering his
confused words with love, but his Father listens with immense
affection and understanding.

V3, p725, L3+4

M 99:11 — The child speaks, and even if his words are
unintelligible they are very much loved; and if he
remained silent, one would be afraid that he might
be dumb.

V3, p725, L5+6

M 99:12 — His folk are happy even when he stammers; they
accept his defect, viewing it with favor, as though
it was glory.

V4, p118, L13+14

M 111:19 — One can never be faulted for speaking of love
about the Beautiful one, for however far his
speaking goes, he would never give you justice.

V4, p118, L15+16

M 111:20 — A child speaks to his father with love, while his
father listens with love to whatever he says.

V4, p118, L17+18

ܘܟܕ ܫܡܥ ܠܗ ܕܐܡ̈ܬܠܐ ܘܡܡܠܠܢ ܠܗ:
ܡܩܒܠ ܠܗܘܢ ܐܝܟ ܗܘ ܕܐܡܪ ܫܪܝܪ̈ܬܐ܀

M 111:21 — And as he hears him speak through images, he accepts them as though by someone speaking serious facts.

V4, p118, L19+20

ܡܠܥܠܥ ܣܓܝܐ ܟܕ ܠܐ ܡܦܪܫ ܡܕܡ ܕܐܡܪ:
ܘܚܕܐ ܒܡܡܠܠܗ ܐܒ ܡܢ ܡܡܠܠܐ ܕܦܝܠܣܘܦ̈ܐ܀

M 111:22 — Even when he stammers a lot without making sense, the father is happier with his speech than with that of philosophers.

V4, p118, L21+22

ܡܕܝܢ ܐܢܐ ܐܝܟ ܛܠܝܐ ܩܕܡ ܐܒܘܗܝ:
ܗܐ ܡܡܠܠ ܐܢܐ ܩܕܡ ܐܠܗܐ ܒܚܘܒܐ ܪܒܐ܀

M 111:23 — Hence I am like a child before his father, Behold, I speak before God with great love.

CONCLUDING REMARKS

So here is our poet, an inspiration to read; a teacher who fathomed his subject, the entire Bible, and appreciated its deep mysteries. He expressed these mysteries in a language full of eloquence, yet one we could understand. He was an illuminator who shed new light on the Biblical narratives and clothed them in robes that we could recognize, using his unique brand of artistry of images and symbols. But while he negotiates his way through all this, he also comes across as a man who is genuinely ready to share with his audience his inner feelings of anxiety, inadequacy and self reproach; he was never aloof. Last but not least, what distinctly comes across is a man who is passionately devoted to one single vocation in life, namely that of revealing the wonders of Creation, and *ihidoyutho* (the Oneness) of the Son with the Father.